Burn Out

Burn Out

My story from burn out to recovery

"Learn lessons from my journey"

Mike Abbott

SUNESIS MINISTRIES LTD

Burn Out: My story from burn out to recovery "Learn lessons from my journey"

Copyright © 2020 Mike Abbott. The right of Mike Abbott to be identified as author of this work has been asserted by him in accordance with the Copyright, Designs, and Patents Act 1988. All rights reserved. No part of this publication may be reproduced or transmitted in any form or by any means, electronic or mechanical, including photocopy, recording, or any information storage and retrieval system, without permission in writing from the author.

ISBN 978-0-9566864-2-8

Published by Sunesis Ministries Ltd. For more information about Sunesis Ministries Ltd, please visit:

www.stuartpattico.com

The author of this book does not dispense medical advice or prescribe the use of any technique as a form of treatment for physical, emotional, or medical problems without the advice of a physician, either directly or indirectly. The intent of the author is only to offer information of a general nature. In the event you use any of the information in this book for yourself, the author and publisher assume no responsibility for your actions.

The views expressed in this book are solely those of the author and do not necessarily reflect the views of the publisher, and the publisher hereby disclaims any responsibility for them.

Contents

FOREWORD	8
DEDICATION	10
ACKNOWLEDGEMENTS	11
CHAPTER ONE: WHAT HAPPENED TO ME?	13
My Background	13
Life in Retail	17
Hours overload	22
The melting point	25
Chapter Summary	26
CHAPTER TWO: HITTING ROCK BOTTOM	28
That life changing day	28
My wife interventions	31
What I couldn't face	35
Feelings of failure	39
Chapter Summary	40
CHAPTER THREE: GETTING OFF THE MERRY-GO-ROUND	41
Forced to take time out	41
How long will it take ?	43
What did I do to assist with my recovery ?	45
On the road to recovery	48
Chapter Summary	50

Chapter Four: Light at the End of the Tunnel — 51

Beginning to feel normal again — 51
A new Job — 52
Coming off anti-depressants medication — 54
Going back to what I do best — 55
Chapter Summary — 57

Chapter Five: Making Crucial Decisions — 59

The danger of doing what other people think is best for you — 59
How do you know what's right for you? — 62
Uniqueness of your journey (and don't lose sight of who you are) — 62
Lessons learnt and what I had to implement — 64
Chapter Summary — 64

Chapter Six: Not neglecting other areas of your life. — 66

Being driven is okay, but not when it's all consuming — 66
Neglecting my space — 69
Re-building my work life balance (safeguards) — 72
Being able to laugh again! — 74
Chapter Summary — 76

Chapter Seven: How to identify when you are near burn out...what the signs are! — 78

My symptoms and warning signs — 78
Effects on my family — 80
Toll on my health and wellbeing — 81
Some symptoms have remained — 82

Chapter Summary	82

CHAPTER EIGHT: TOOLS TO GET BACK UP! 84

CHAPTER NINE: MAKING SURE YOU GET THE RIGHT MENTOR 89

My experience of working with different mentors (Good & ugly)	89
My views on finding the right mentor	93
The world needs mentors	94
Being a mentor to others (My non-negotiable)	96
Chapter Summary	97

CHAPTER TEN: HOPE FOR YOUR FUTURE 98

My life now compared to what it was.	98
Making that choice - today's the day.	100
Your Future days	101
Chapter Summary	102

Foreword

I have had the privilege of knowing Mike Abbott for around 15 years personally as his Pastor and friend. He has a passion for life and for success. Whatever Mike does in life he does it well. It takes this level of commitment to be successful, yet this often leads to burnout.

In an ever-changing world, where life moves at 200 miles an hour, burnout within individuals and society is even more common, and sadly the devastating effects that it leaves, not only on the individual, but family friends and work colleges. I witnessed first-hand Mike's own burnout and saw its traumatic and shattering effects upon him, his family, and the lengthy period it took him to recover.

Mike has brilliantly captured it within the pages of this book, his very distinctive and refreshing account will leave you inspired. You will be laughing one minute and crying the next, as you read his frank and captivating story. His message is clear that he does not want anyone else to suffer what he went through and more importantly, what are the lessons and tools that will enable you to avoid experiencing burnout, or getting back on your feet.

I highly recommend Mike's book and suggest that you use it as a stepping stone to avoid the costly effects of burnout.

Andrew White
Senior Pastor Victory Gospel Church

Dedication

I dedicate this book to my beautiful wife Pauline, who stood by me with her unwavering love and commitment towards myself, during those dark days of my burnout.

Acknowledgments

I wish to acknowledge the many incredible people that have loved, cared and stood by me over the years.

To my wonderful parents, Norman and Joan, whose love, commitment and support have always been there from the time I entered planet earth, having embraced some of my crazy adventures along the way!

My sister Claire who has a heart as big as the ocean and beyond.

Pauline, the love of my life for your love, friendship, laughter and sense of adventure. And of course, our two girls, Tiger Lilly and Esther Joy (4 legged daughters)

Ann, for your phone calls of support and encouragement.

Peter and Gail, for your faithfulness and support to me, now getting on towards 40 years.

Roger, the brother that I never had, for your fun and

laughter.

Andrew, thanks for your love and support during my darkest days and for being there at the end of the phone.

Bishop Wayne, my business mentor, role model and friend. Whose incredible business insights have empowered me to see the world with a new pair of glasses.

Ahmed, thank you for your patience and support with the template, pictures, and computer skills for this book.

Lilly, my editor, for your insights, guidance and advice on getting the best out of me.

Simon, for your incredible book design and support.

Finally, I want to acknowledge all the other unsung heroes who have encouraged, strengthened and been there for me.

1

What happened to me?

MY BACKGROUND

Well, I can't believe how fast my life has passed me by; it doesn't seem possible that I will soon be entering my sixtieth year! So how did I arrive at this junction in my life and where has my life taken me? Well, I think it's important to start at the very beginning.

Born at Hillingdon Hospital, on 21st August 1961, in the early hours - a boy, to my parent's joy, I grew up in West London, in a small town called Ruislip Manor. Two years later, my sister Claire was born and life began in the West London suburb, near the Metropolitan line. My parents, Norman and Joan came originally from North London. My father, from Kings Cross and my mother, from Highbury & Islington. They decided once they got married, back in 1960, that they would move out of central London and settle in a residence in the suburbs that would be their first home, a two up two down terraced house. As they set up home, they did not have a lot of money and the furniture was either a deck-chair or a sofa that had seen better days.

I have fond memories of growing up in a street where the neighbours supported each other and would often have dinner parties, celebrating someone's birthday and other events. We played with the kids and would often go around the back to play in their gardens, climbing trees and imagining that we were cowboys and Indians - crazy, but fun.

We even went to the same holiday locations as our neighbours, Cornwall, and the wonderful town of St Austell. Packing up the car, which was an old Ford Popular two door, my sister and I used to sleep in the back of the car, on a makeshift bed, as my father drove on our way down to Cornwall for two weeks of sea, sun and fun. Invariably, the weather was such a bit hit and miss. I loved body surfing and riding the waves; it was such fun and excitement. One had to be respectful of the sea as it was extremely rough and the strong currents could soon whisk you quickly out, way beyond your swimming abilities, at any moment. My dad was particularly aware of the lifeguard flags and posts and would always be telling us not go in if the flag was red, which stood for no swimming. Sadly, many people did not obey the warnings, and over the years many strong swimmers lost their lives. He also loved to take us crabbing and seeing the sea life in the rock pools. And then we would return back to home with fond memories of the long summer evenings, and if the weather had been kind to us, amazing times on the beach.

My junior years at school were happy and content, nothing seemed to be too much pressure, but I did struggle with Maths and English. My report stated, "Michael is a pleasant child that easily gets distracted"!! And then there was secondary school, which in those days was called Southbourne Comprehensive, and oh boy, this was a complete shock from the Junior School. You were put in sets according to your

What happened to me?

ability for Maths and English, which were along the lines of - Top set, second set, third set and fourth set. And then you had the Michael Abbott set - the remedial set, where all the supposed dim wits ended up. This set were the ones that the school didn't know what to do with and so were just put there. It was a class and world all of its own, with one teacher taking you for Maths and English, while for all other subjects, like cooking and woodwork, you would be re-joining the other pupils. No one was interested in learning in this set, and the teacher who was a nice guy, didn't really have a clue what to do with us. But when it came to handling a class of what the world would call useless, and without a future, then it was a case of 'let's do something with them, just to pass the time of day'. It makes my blood boil thinking about it now and I am so thankful that schools have come a long way since.

So, my school years flew by and then, what was I going to do? Well, I was good at music, cooking and making people laugh. After consulting with a Careers Advisor and my parents, of course. I decided to go to Westminster catering college in Victoria, London, to do my City and Guilds in catering. I loved cooking, but being shouted at by the chefs was not a pleasant experience, and after one year, I decided that being a chef was not for me. So, my wonderful mother, who happened to work in the same establishment, got me a job as a post boy, for Audits of Great Britain. After doing this I then joined the army as a musician, in the staff band of the Royal Army Ordnance Corps, where I played the clarinet. I personally think that my dad did a deal with the army and got a back hander - he never disclosed the sum he received!! I did nine years' service, and left, as I didn't want to do twenty-two years and then have to readjust into "civvie street", to find a job and start over again.

Coming out of the army after nine years, was tough enough and as much as they tried to prepare you for life outside, it was a big shock. This was because everything in the army was thought through for you, as there were strict rules in order to get things done. My first job was a van driver for a print finishing company and I delivered the finished jobs to companies around the Hampshire, Surrey and surrounding areas. Then after a while, I left and got a job in direct sales, selling fire extinguishers. My patch was in Central London, and after a week's intense training course, every day I had to go door to door, trying to get people to buy. The target was two fire extinguishers and two service contracts per day. This was at the sharp end of selling, deep down at the coal face. If you didn't succeed in hitting your targets, you were out. I hated it, absolutely hated all the rejection. I ended up just going into a shop and instead of asking them to buy a fire extinguisher, I would end up buying a bar of chocolate, or a suit!!!

So, after three months, I was unemployed. This was the first time since I had left school that I had no income and no employment. After going to the job center and doing various temporary jobs, I applied and got on the management training scheme of Allders of Camberley, a department store, based in Camberley, with stores in the south of England. I did this for two and half years, before being made redundant. Again, I was out of work, doing all I could to make ends meet. Parcel force was my next job as a delivery driver, before becoming one of their depot trainers, delivering NVQs to the staff.

By this time, I had been married to a wonderful lady called Pauline, and we set up home in north Hampshire. Then in 1996 we moved to Southampton, Hampshire. I then had to find new work and got a job with a major supermarket, as a training manager, in one of their large superstores. Throughout the remainder of this book, this supermarket will be referred to as "the Company"

LIFE IN RETAIL

The Company was a whole new ball game, completely different to anything that I have ever experienced in my working life. Retail is manic, a full on twenty-four-seven, hour job. The store employed four hundred and fifty staff, and is a massive operation, fast paced and so demanding. The stores' biggest trading day was a Sunday, in which it took over one hundred thousand pounds, and a staggering weekly sales figure of one point two million pounds!

Learning how they wanted you to serve customers and fill the store when deliveries were inevitably late, my role was to do inductions for every new starter who joined the company, and every Saturday for nearly six and a half years, I would be running one, as well as keeping training alive within the store. This included telling them about the company's history and what we expected of them. The Company had exceptionally high standards in everything that it set out to do - training, customer loyalty and the philosophy that the customer was always right, were drummed into you. It was a very fast pace industry to work in.

Christmas and peak seasonal times were like being hit by a train going at two hundred miles an hour. Christmas is full on, it is crazy. I had never seen anything like it in my life - customers with trolleys so full that they could hardly push them around the store. Some were really nice and then there were the ones who were so rude and demanding, shouting in your face, screaming, and then saying that they were going to report you to all and sundry.

My fellow managers took some time to get to know me - this outsider, who had come in to make sure department training was completed, and to make sure that they had personal development plans. It took a while for them to accept me and to see that I was not the enemy.

I have to say that the training I received from the Company was brilliant. There were training courses I had never heard of, such as personal development plan, assertiveness training, time management, team work, having difficult conversations - and all of this was to enable you to work on areas in your life that you hadn't realized needed working on - they called it your blind side. And then there were the famous Key Performance Indicators. Then, when you thought you had got it, blow me down, they rolled out another way of doing things. They were always trying new and continued improvement, as they stated - the new way forward. If you didn't like it or didn't adapt to change, then you were soon gone, and replaced by someone more willing to conform to their ways of doing things.

The hours were long and demanding and this was no nine to five job that I had previously done, as I was expected to work on past scheduled hours for free!! Or as they put it, "It's for your own development". The times that I heard this over the years, if I had patented this saying, I could have made a fortune!

I did have some great times as well and the work mates and colleagues made it worthwhile. I worked with some amazing people, such as store managers who were brilliant, and we laughed at the customers behind their backs. I'm grateful for the training and work ethic that the Company gave me that has stood with me since leaving.

I was placed onto the management training program, to become a personnel manager. After that, I was then placed onto management courses which I would be required to have completed and finished, to ensure that I was of the right calibre which was required. This was not something that was handed to you on a plate, you had to go and get it.

The rounds of interviews and selection days/boards, were demanding, to say the least. My past job experiences proved to be very helpful and I was given a twelve-week placement as a personnel manager, covering all aspects of human resources, from recruitment, training and everything in between. It was more like being an agony aunt, and being a man in a female world was eye-opening, to say the least.

I think I could have written a column in the Sun newspaper, answering the situations and stories of the staff's lives. Wow! I have dealt with so much over the twenty years that I worked for the Company - people dying, people being terminally ill, sexual harassment cases, stealing and everything else in between. It certainly opened my eyes to a world that was new to me, and really made me appreciate the wonderful family that I had been blessed with. So, I eventually passed the training and became a personnel manager, a Multi-site manager, covering stores in Berkshire, Hampshire, Wiltshire and the USA, for a short secondment. At the time, my line manager, who was a personnel group manager, and who covered the region in which I worked, said that if I wanted to get to the next level on the management ladder, I would have to become a work level three, as I was a work level two. In order to do the job that she did, the best way to do this was, by way of becoming a store manager. I told her that she had lost the plot and as long as I had breath, I would never become one!!! She kept saying at my annual reviews, the same message, and this went on for some years. Back and forth we would go, me across one side of the table and her the other. And the more direct I would get! But after realising that there was no other option, and I think I must have had a brain transplant, and certainly lost my marbles, I agreed to yet again undertaking the necessary training to become a store manager in the Company!!!!

Another round of training and this time I had to do it whilst performing my other job as a personnel manager, following a training needs analysis, completing each task and training and getting each part signed off. Then there was another sign on panel, and work shadowing other managers who had been in the job a long time.

My store director at the time, decided to put me in a store with fifty staff and at the time, with a ninety-five thousand to one hundred thousand pounds weekly turnover. This was on a twelve-week placement, having reviews every four weeks with my store director, being measured against the Key Performance Indicators (KPIs) and running the shop. Well, it's okay doing your training in a store that runs smoothly, and working alongside someone who has had the full and correct training, but I was now the person in charge, who everyone expected to know the answers. I was assigned to another nearby store manager who was my mentor, who would come in and keep an eye on me, pointing out things that I was not doing right. I was now line manager to the person who was previously my personnel manager. It was a steep learning curve.

What happened to me?

I had been in my placement for twelve weeks and a little bit more, when during the last week, the store director came in to see me unannounced. He informed me that I was being removed from the store as the twelve-week placement had come to an end. He was not putting me forward to be signed off and I was to be leaving with immediate effect. That day was my last. He also said that I had not learnt the technical side of the job quickly enough and that although my leadership skills were up to the mark, I was out, with someone else replacing me the next day. I was then given the choices of going back to being a personnel manager, or to be a store manager in a smaller format, or as a store manager, on the training programs for this format and start again!!

I was in complete shock. I didn't know what to say and mumbled a reply. I had to tell him my decision by the following Monday. He left, without a word of thanks for what I had achieved. I had done my best, really tried, but I had failed. After discussing this with my wife and a close friend, I decided I had come too far to go back to being a personnel manager. I would move across to the new format and start again and become a store manager in its new format. So, yet again, I was work shadowing an experienced manager, and completing my training course and my Technical needs analysis (TNA). I was then placed in a store on my placement, with this time only fourteen staff, including two team leaders and a deputy manager.

Hours overload

The store was in a tough location. Opening hours were seven days a week, Monday to Sunday, six in the morning to ten in the evening. The team was not well settled and was dysfunctional. The leadership consisted of myself, as store manager, a deputy manager and two team leaders. Clear lines of responsibilities were not in place and they did not get on at all with each other. The team leaders didn't respect the deputy and there were petty arguments. It was up to me to try to keep all parties happy.

One of the major differences in this format was that you were expected to do all the jobs, and be up to speed. For example, before the store would open, you had to run around the store and ensure that all the prices on the items were correct, allowing for changes in prices. Then there was taking in the deliveries and unloading and re-load the lorries in all-weather conditions. The store was on the main road, and the

What happened to me?

lorries had to unload there. This was very inconvenient as we were located among a row of shops that included a betting office. Pundits would park their cars and not come out of the betting office until they had run out of money. Well, trying to get them to move so that we could unload the lorries was impossible, as they would refuse in a very aggressive manner, making you know that they had every right to be in there. It was hopeless, absolutely hopeless. The lorries would be stuck on the road blocking the flow of traffic, with nowhere to go, customers wanting products that were on the lorry that we could not unload, and this happened day in, day out - it was a living nightmare.

Having come from a shop that had fifty staff where you could have your breaks and lunch breaks, to now, having no breaks, or eating your lunch on the go, was so full on. It was never-ending and as you never had all fourteen of the staff at any one time, it always seemed to be such a fight. It was a never-ending circle, and of course, I was on placement, still having to go through the four-weekly reviews and with the dreaded sign off panel to pass, before I could be appointed and earn the salary that went with the job.

I, of course was running around like a headless chicken. We had till shorts, as some member of staff was stealing. So, there would be phone calls to find out why there was yet another till short. Of course, I would be reminded that I was the store's manager and needed to sort it out, with the warning of the sign off panel to come, which I needed to pass. This was more pressure and the pressures continued to mount with every new passing day.

The management team opened and closed the shop, which meant there was the overload of hours that I was doing every day. If the person who was running the late shift didn't come in, or phoned in sick …… you've guessed it. I as the store manager, would be frantically phoning other stores in the areas to get cover, even though we were all in the same boat. If I phoned my line manager, he would ask what I expected him to do about it, with the reminder that I was in charge and responsible.

Because I felt responsible and was wanting to show that I could run a store, and wanted to pass my sign off panel, I ended up working sixteen-hour days, covering the deputy manger's or team leader's hours. This went on week in week out, with no breaks. I was now working sixty to eighty hours a week, instead of my scheduled thirty hours. Doing this for seven days a week, it began to start taking its toll on me. I started having panic attacks. I would phone Pauline up, saying that I'm failing. I could hear the despair in her voice, as she didn't know how to help, or she felt so helpless at the other end of the phone. I kept saying over and over again, 'I don't know what to do.'

I would walk out of the store and down a side alley and cry - no one was watching me. I felt so alone and just didn't know what to do. I started shaking and feeling sick. I felt so trapped and all I could hear in my head was, "You're a failure Mike Abbott, you're a failure Mike Abbott, you're a failure Mike Abbott, your life is useless".

I would phone other friends and work colleagues; I was so alone, so, so, alone. I still kept going every day, trying to put on a brave face to the other staff, and yet inside I was crying. I was getting little or no sleep, tossing and turning, worrying about the next day, the next day coming home and telling my wife that I was a failure, and useless.

This went on for weeks and weeks. Our relationship was suffering, and we would row. My wife would make suggestions which I just couldn't grasp and she became worried about me. I remember going to my nephew's twenty-first birthday party. It was a family celebration, where we would all be gathering to celebrate this. We were to meet in a pub in Ruislip Manor, called JJ Moons, on a Saturday night. I was supposed to be finishing early, to get away to drive the hour and half from Southampton, to be there in time. Yet again, there was some delay or other in my leaving work, which meant rushing home to get changed and the mad dash to get there in time.

When we arrived at the pub, my family didn't greet me as they normally would, like 'Great to see you Mike', and have a laugh and banter. But this time, they looked at me and said, 'Mike you look awful …… I'm really worried about you …… please, please go and see a doctor.' It was not just one member of my family; both my father and mother took me to one side to ask if I was okay. Then, without my knowing, my dad spoke to Pauline, asking her what was going on - he was so concerned. Later that same evening, I received a phone call from the store. Yet again, my down time had been interrupted by work. I couldn't even have time for a special occasion without the 'rope' of urgency, pulling me back to the store, some seventy miles away.

THE MELTING POINT

We returned home from what should have been a wonderful celebration, which was now ruined by work. The car journey home was yet again back into the theme of "your family are worried about you Mike, they care, you need to listen to them……"

Yes, I knew, but they were not living in my world; they didn't work in retail with all the demands. And again, I was back at work the following Monday. This time my panic attacks got worse and worse, and lasted longer. I just could not cope with the melting pot of despair that I was in. I was at the bottom of the pot, and I just didn't know how to climb back up and out into a world that I was sinking further and further into.

The phone calls to my wife and friends were now at desperation point, daily and hourly at times.

During this time there was a store manager called Steve, who came across and saw me, he was a superstar. But although he was supportive, he was not living inside my mind and bless him, he tried - he kept saying, 'You can do this Mike, you can do this Mike'. But it was too late, I kept going and going, day in, week out. I just didn't want to be a failure again.

CHAPTER SUMMARY

- Amazing parents who always did their best for me and my sister
- Junior school that was wonderful
- Secondary school classed me as remedial
- Teacher who didn't know how to help me
- Love of cooking but not treatment of chefs
- Mother finds me a new job
- Army life and doing music

What happened to me?

- Adjusting to life after the army
- A number of different jobs
- Retail
- Panic attacks and their toll

2

Hitting Rock Bottom

THAT LIFE CHANGING DAY

I remember it being a Monday morning, early. The house was in complete darkness. No one was outside starting their vehicles, or making a sound …… that strange eerie sound of the wind tapping at the windows, combined with the seagulls making their customary cries and yelps…..

I was getting ready to go to work as I had done week in week out, like a prize fighter still willing to drag his body through hell and back, to beat his opponent and gain the winner's prize.

The dawn of another day, but this new day was to be like no other I have experienced since, or would wish upon my worst enemy. Another week was staring at me, like a bleak cold winter's night - Bleakness and Darkness, were their names.

I felt like I was in a dream. I was on a never-ending merry-go-round, where the fairground owner was laughing at me, as I went around and around again. His laughs and chuckles getting louder as I passed him with each completion of the circuit. Seeing the gleam and smirks of amusement riding across his face, he had decided not to switch the ride off, (my one pound for three minutes, should have been well and truly over) and then seeing me still on, and the music churning away, it seemed that he had gone elsewhere for the night and was never going to return, until the new dawn or until he had slept off his hangover.

I had showered and somehow managed to get myself dressed. My mind and body were pulling at me in completely different directions, like a Christmas cracker, with two individuals, holding each side and fighting over who was the stronger, and neither side willing to let go until.....

And then as I crept back into the bedroom, I was trying not wake my wife Pauline, as she was having a lie in. The bedroom lights were off and I sat on the edge of the bed. I opened my mouth and words tumbled out, but I was not making sense at all. Pauline stirred and asked me what was wrong, but still I could not get my words to make any sense. I continued sitting on the bed and I was no longer in control of my words or of any of my bodily functions. I was shaking, crying uncontrollably and couldn't talk sense.

Pauline started crying and saying, 'You're not going in, are you? You're not going in.....you're not going to work.....how can you go like this? How can you go like this and function? Please tell me. Come on Mike, answer me.' By this time, she was shouting as she had gotten louder and louder with each new breath.

Still, I just sat there for what seemed like an eternity, not able to converse with her or to be able to answer her questions. She got out of bed and put her arms around me, saying, 'Mike, Mike, Mike, Mike.' Throughout our married life we had always tried to talk and work things through. I will say at this point that it was not always like that. We married in our thirties and had previously lived separately, with very independent lives. After our honeymoon and several months in, it seemed that all we did was argue, over such stupid and trivial things. We were extremely opinionated, strong willed and feisty, and when we fought it was .....oh boy..... like a fight until the death.

The first year we had to go and get some marriage counselling to aid us with our communication skills, or to be more frank – mine, otherwise our marriage would have crumbled and been anther government static. So, here we were now, with some fifteen years or more having passed since this point and junction in our married life.

And all my efforts to communicate and express what was

occurring, was not happening for me. My speech was failing me. My body had shut down like a hot air balloon, with its helium air now fully delating, with the wind blowing in the whatever new direction it wanted. Oh, oh.....what was happening to me? I was so scared and frightened. Such dreadful thoughts were racing through my mind. Was I having a heart attack? Was this it? My life now over ...... gone ..... gone ...... gone. Mike Abbott's existence on planet earth...time done. No goodbyes.

Pauline continued to hold me tightly in her arms, as our tears streamed down our faces, our tears now intertwining and mingling together, like a river does, as it enters into the ocean, having reached it final destination and merging into one. This was a life changing day which I was never ever going to forget.

My wife interventions

Pauline put me into the bed, still fully clothed, and pulled the duvet over me. She was in total control mode, telling me to stay there as she was going to phone the doctor and get me an appointment, and if need be, would go down to the surgery herself. The true Yorkshire farmer's daughter was now in full throttle, like a beautiful Dexter tractor, humming at full speed...in full control and woe betide anyone that got in its way, or hers.

Those were the days when you phoned your local doctor and could get an appointment the same morning, not like it is now, where you have to go through this awful queuing system, to then have a triage nurse phone you back, and then you have to go through your symptoms, like being crossed examined in the witness box of the Old Bailey, before you can eventually get an appointment. She returned from the surgery to inform me that we had got an appointment with my doctor. She told me that she was taking me to see him, and that from now on, I was going to have to listen to her as she was in total control now. Pauline reminded me that I had not listened to her all these months. Now, I had no choice as my life and health were more important. She was laying down the law. My wife continued, that she was also going to be phoning my boss to tell him what had happened. She didn't care whether or not I wanted her to, and rushed off to make the call.

Pauline drove me to the GP's surgery. Sitting in the waiting room, I just kept looking at the floor. I was totally wrecked, my mind and body, screaming at me. We were eventually summoned in to see the GP. As I sat there looking at him, he asked me what was wrong. He didn't move, just waited for my response. He was different today - his voice was so calm and he looked concerned. I still could not talk and continued to mumble. Pauline interjected and explained what had happened, and described the events leading up to this moment. She did not hold back, she was like a bag of popcorn that was in the microwave popping with every new sentence and information that proceeded out of her mouth.

He paused, after listening so carefully without any interruptions, which was not like him. Then he said that I was totally and completely burned out. If I had not gone to see him, he continued, and had carried on working in the same way, I would have had a nervous breakdown which I would have never recovered from. He did not mince his words. He signed me off work for fourteen days, and then I was to return and see him, before he would allow me to go back to work.

Pauline thanked him for his kindness and understanding of the situation and promised that she would ensure that I got some rest, and would see him with myself in a fortnight's time.

My symptoms certainly matched those as described in an article by Kohok[1]. I would agree that these factors were occurring in my life as stated in the extract below:

> "The World Health Organisation, has now officially recognised burnout as an occupational phenomenon, describing it as a "syndrome resulting from chronic workplace stress that has not been successfully managed". It is characterised by feelings of exhaustion, negativism or cynicism related to one's job and poor performance. However, it can be hard for people to understand what's wrong."

I think it's quite difficult to identify your own signs of burnout. "People close to you, or managers, are very good at identifying it from the other side," says Dr Rachel Morris, a GP who, over fifteen years, saw many patients who were ill because of workplace stress. She says, "Patients suffering from burnout may become unsure of themselves, feel cynical, hopeless or detached, stop eating properly, and feel continually tired. They may also feel angry or resentful about work, or towards colleagues and friends[1]"

The organization, Frontiers in Psychology goes further,

---

[1] Kohok, S. (2019), Are you burning out? BBC World Service

stating[2]:

"Work-related chronic stress is a major health challenge in Western societies. The World Health Organization assumes work stress as a growing health risk for both the individual and the society[3]. Within the German Health Interview and Examination Survey for Adults (DEGS1) conducted between 2008 and 2011, 11% of the 5,850 participants between 18 And 64 years reported high levels of chronic stress. Higher levels occurred for woman than for men and for those with lower socio-economic status (Hapkeetal et al.,2013). One phenomenon often described in connection with chronic stress at work is burnout. Burnout was originally attributed to the field of social work, arguing that employees of the social work sector may develop burnout due to the highly emotional demands of client-work[4].

We left the doctor's surgery and returned home. I was still not able to speak or function as I normally would be doing. The car was back on our drive, with me now facing two weeks

---

[2] Fleischhauer, M., Miller, R., Magdalena Katharina, W., Marlene, P., Clemens, K., and Sören. E., (2019) Thinking Against Burnout? An Individual's Tendency to Engage in and Enjoy Thinking as a Potential Resilience Factor of Burnout Symptoms and Burnout-Related Impairment in Executive Functioning.

[3] Leka, S., and Jain, A. (2010). Health Impact of Psychosocial Hazards at Work: An Overview. Geneva: World Health Organizatio Hapke, U., Maske, U., Scheidt-Nave, C., Bode, L., Schlack, R., and Busch, M. (2013).

[4] Maslach, C., and Jackson, S. E. (1981). The measurement of experienced burnout. J. Organ. Behav. 2, 99–113. doi: 10.1002/job.4030020205

without doing anything.

We had a caravan in Somerset that we could get away to. Pauline took herself and our two Jack Russells down there to set up, and after a day, she came back to get me. As I needed to get away from it all, the caravan was ideal, as it was in the middle of nowhere, on a farmer's field. No phone connections and no WiFi! Pauline would be in her element, pigs, sheep, goats, donkeys and in the rural countryside...and the peacocks, with their beautiful feathers. I'm not sure what class of animal she would have put me in, or category - probably a stubborn billy goat......

She returned and packed me into the car. I was now a detainee in her care, fully under her control, and had to follow her orders, but not like my old sergeant major, barking orders and screaming at me in my basic training. This time he had been replaced by her loving care and attention to my wellbeing. This was her total focus.

WHAT I COULDN'T FACE

We were facing a two-hour journey down in the car to Somerset, via the M27 and A35. There was no question of me driving as I couldn't face dealing with all that traffic. I just wanted to get there as quickly as possible. On the way, we had to stop off at a supermarket in Bridport to get supplies for the two weeks that we were going to be there. As I got out of the car and entered the store, I froze and could not face going into the store... the crowds of people and the noise...all I wanted to do was use the toilet and get out, returning to the safety of our car. I was sinking inside and feeling sick. The walls of the store felt like they were crowding in on me and wanting to suffocate me, their walls grabbing at my neck, screaming .....It was like I was experiencing a scary attraction at Disneyland, or I was in an Alfred Hitchcock horror film, or in the Boston Strangler, now renamed for my purposes, The Bridport Strangler - the title of his new film, Mike Abbott, with the leading role....

People were looking at me, and staring at me. Oh I hated it, really hated it. I wanted to say something back to them. I looked back at them with the stern look of a madman, someone not to be messed with. But this had been my arena, my place of work, although a different chain and company. This was retail and had been my life since 2007, my place of comfort and I knew how it operated. I wanted to run away as far as possible, into a cave and never come out. My head was spinning and it was a dark, lonely place. Yes, I had the love and support of my beautiful wife. But I never wanted to go back out again into this cruel world.

'Please get me to the caravan and let's shut the door, and I can be there for the next two weeks,' I told Pauline. 'You do the shopping, I can't cope, I can't cope.' She returned with the shopping, and again we were on our way to the campsite. After getting out of the car and hurrying into the van, I didn't want to speak to fellow holiday-makers and left Pauline to get everything out of the car. 'Tell them, I'm not well and to leave me well alone,' I said to her, then I laid down on the bed and went to sleep. And that's all I did for the next two weeks, sleep and sleep and more sleep. I mean sleep for fourteen hours at night, get up have breakfast and then go back to sleep, have dinner and then sleep... all day, every day, for two weeks. I never went anywhere, talked to anyone, just ate and slept. Pauline did everything. I barely spoke to her, or interacted with our two dogs.

Hitting Rock Bottom

Then the two weeks were up and I was having to report back to my GP and tell him of my progress and to see if I was ready to go back to work. Just before we went back, Pauline wanted to go into the local town and get some shopping and have a bite to eat at a local café. I agreed and duly went, taking the two dogs with us. The weather was kind and we were able to find a spot outside the restaurant. One of our dogs, Toby, kept barking at everyone that passed him by, he just wanted to say hello. I just sat there, looked after the two dogs, while Pauline ordered the food and then we ate. The plan was that once we had finished eating, that Pauline would get some shopping from the local Lidl, and we would return to the caravan, and then in a few days' time would be returning back home, to Southampton.

Pauline had gone off shopping leaving me with the dogs, and out came two old ladies, who were extremely posh. They had eaten their meals inside the café. As they passed me, they commented that our dogs had ruined their dinner by their continual barking. Well, I just rose up and started shouting at them at the top of my voice. I didn't hold back. On and on I went. I was screaming at them, screaming in their faces. They looked terrified and the owner of the café came running out. He got in between me and the two old ladies, and told me if I didn't calm down that he would have to call the police. This was so outside of my charter and disposition. I was losing it completely - I had no safety barriers or bumpers to bounce me back to my senses. It was like I was now driving a bumper car at the fair, ramming everyone who came across my path. With these two old ladies within my sight, it was like my car was hitting them instead of a bumper. Now, with my verbal abuse and outrage, I didn't care, I was totally out of control in my reactions and they hurried away. They left in total shock and horror, looking completely shell shocked. By this time Pauline had returned, wondering what on earth had been going on in her absence.

She took me back to the caravan and again I was like a zombie, until we had to return home.

FEELINGS OF FAILURE

The total horror and realization of my actions towards these two old ladies floated passed me as I tried to drift off to sleep. I was now so lost and felt a complete failure. Why had I failed and was this new pattern of behavior going to be here for the rest of my life? I then began to think about the past year or so. I could not even manage and lead a team of staff as store manager with fifty staff. My store director said, *'I'm removing you.'* Those thoughts were getting louder and louder in my mind, sounding like the waves crashing against the shore, hitting the rocks as they went back and forth and bellowing as they splashed: **Mike Abbott you are a failure.......**

Then there was the move to the smaller format within the Company. *'You can't manage and get signed off.'* Was it me? Had I done something wrong? Where it had all gone so wrong? I had so wanted to progress within the company and move up the corporate ladder. I then thought back to my school years, *'remedial'* ...what a great label I now was.

I had failed my wife by not listening and heading her warnings. The burden I had placed upon her, phoning her up continually and saying I was a failure, had placed such a strain upon our marriage. It went on and on. Then there were my close family, my parents and the rest of my family and friends who said, 'Mike you cannot continue like this. You're not listening to your body. You're not getting any younger.' I saw all my effort and hard work disappearing before my very eyes. I had lost status, and now having to tell them that they were right, was so, so humiliating, and now, them having to repeat the same message over and over again.

I had no choice but to go back to the doctor upon returning home. And of course, Pauline came with me - she was there at each difficult stage. I cannot put into words, and express fully without getting emotional even today, my love and gratitude for her unwavering love and commitment to me. She went through hell living with me in those first few weeks, but she never complained or moaned, but faithfully stood there by my side. Again, the loneliness I felt inside gripped me and was now my cloud, one of complete failure. All these times that I had failed had now grouped together in the sky above my head. They were black and there were no rays of sunshine outside of them. They just blocked the sun. Hope had now evaporated into a time beyond. My fate awaited in the hands of the doctor.

Chapter Summary

- My body shut down and told me it had enough of the toll I had placed upon it.
- That life changing day will ever be etched on my mind, for the rest of my days.
- The unconditional, amazing love of my wife Pauline. Without her intervention, I would not be functioning as I am today.
- The amazing doctor who listened so intently upon my first visit after my melt down
- The old ladies that I never had the opportunity to apologies to for my appalling behavior.
- My amazing family and friends - Steve, who stood by me in such dark days. I cannot express my love and thanks enough.

3

Getting off the Merry-Go-Round

FORCED TO TAKE TIME OUT

I was now back in the same surgery where it had all started the previous two weeks, as I entered in to see the doctor. My mind raced before me, trying to figure out what he was going to say, wondering which route he would be taking, with Pauline now in control.

He asked me how I had got on and was delighted on discovering that we had escaped and got away from it all. I replied that all I did was sleep, eat and even more sleep. He asked how I was coping with life in general and was I ready to go back to work and put myself under more pressure.

He wisely asked Pauline first, if she thought I was ready.

Pauline, as I was now realizing, was not going to hold back, regardless of who was in front of her. She is a formidable, lady who once she gets the bit between her teeth, is like a Jack Russell - fiercely loyal and extremely protective of its owner. She relayed that I slept for hours and hours, rising to eat and then sleeping more. She had to do everything, the cooking, looking after the dogs and me. It had been full on - she was not complaining but being real, as this is how she lives.

She then recalled the incident that occurred at the café in Crewkerne, a small town in Somerset, where we had been enjoying a nice lunch sitting outside, as the weather had been kind to us. She went on to describe how upon returning from shopping, she was now witnessing what could have been a scene from EastEnders. It was as if the café had now turned into the Queen Vic, and the tranquil town of Crewkerne, had now become Albert Square in London's East End. Mike Abbott, her once placid easy-going husband had now turned into Phil Mitchell, wanting to take on anyone who got in his way. She recalled how shocked and appalled she was and that had it not been for the intervention of the café owner, I would have been arrested.

The GP leaned back in his chair and then looked at me. He paused and then said, 'Well, it's clear to me that you are not ready to go back to work and you need something to assist you.'
He continued, 'You need a mild anti-depressant to help and assist with your mood swings and to calm you down.'

I was lost for words. I didn't want to go on them at all. I heard of people and stories of people being stuck on them for years. Once you got started, that was it.

He said that he would sign me off work for a further two weeks and would give me the mildest anti-depressant. I was to see him again in two weeks' time. He told me to go away and think about taking them, but warned that I could come off them once, and only once I was better, with his advice and support.

We left the surgery and headed home, I was now being forced to take time off from work to recuperate, and had to think about taking anti-depressants. The car, I was later to discover, would be knowing this route without any map or sat nav to guide it. It could have driven itself there and booked in for a MOT.

I had been so proud up until this point in my career at the Company, because of the little time that I had taken off over the years. Yes, there had been the odd cold, but I was now entering my third week away from work. What would people and my line manager be thinking, as well as the staff in the store and my work colleagues?

No, Pauline was not even allowing me to phone in and speak with my line manager and update him on my progress. It was like I was now Lennie Small from John Steinbeck's classic book[5]. Lennie was a mentally disabled, but gigantic and physically strong man who travels with George as his constant companion. He dreams of "living off the fatta' the lan'" and being able to tend to rabbits. Pauline now became like George Milton (this was not set in the depression, but in the twenty-first century), taking care of Mike (Lennie). After much discussion with other friends, I ended up going on the anti-depressants.

How long will it take?

Back we went down to the caravan, re-loading our supplies

---

[5] Steinbeck, J. (2000) Of Mice and Men: London: Publishing. Penguin Books Ltd.

and following the same procedure that we had done before. Pauline warned me that if we went back out into the local town, that she wasn't leaving me unattended! Great. I was under house arrest. I then got to thinking on how long it was going to take me to fully recover and get back to normality. I hated not being able to know the time frame so that I could be thinking clearly about having my life back again. When could I return to work and get signed off and appointed as a store manager, onwards and up wards within my career, to then move back to becoming a group personnel manager, looking after the HR, and Store Managers and personnel managers for up to twenty stores?

I was not the easiest patient. Pauline had the patience of a saint. More sleep and rest. It was now becoming a pattern that I would be following for the weeks and months ahead. Again, being down in the middle of nowhere, my fellow companions apart from the holiday-makers were, a donkey called Hamish and a bow donkey called Robin. With a small hut serving as the toilet and shower, we had to walk across the field to get water. Thankfully, we were able to connect the electrics via a cable to get the electricity working. Otherwise it would have been back to basics - and I do need my creature comforts.

I had no idea what day it was, as the days seemed to just roll from one into another. Another day and then night went by. I lost track also of time and of course I kept away from people. They were still the enemy. However, was I going to recover?

It came to the time to once again see the doctor, after my now fourth week of being off work.

Getting off the Merry-Go-Round

This time, my usual doctor had been replaced by a female doctor. Again, we had to start all over, explaining what had occurred. She was very sympathetic and suggested a wide range of options that were available to assist me in getting back to work. She signed me off for a further two weeks and said I needed longer to recover in order to be able to return to work. She also wanted to see me in another two weeks' time. 'You've got to be joking,' I said. 'No, I'm not joking', the doctor replied. 'I have your best interest at heart.' I thought she had been in conspiracy with Pauline and had signed a secret pact. What bribes had Pauline also given her and the NHS! It was no contesting with two strong-minded women, who had joined sides and were now ensuring that they were in control, joined up at the hip. They were modern day Emmeline Pankhursts, **who** founded the Women's Social and Political Union, which used militant tactics to agitate for women's suffrage. They were now using their militant campaign on me to alleviate me from my suffering and mental torment!

The feeling of shock still showed on my face, like an old hamster that I once had, running endlessly and going nowhere on its hamster wheel. Hamsters, as you know, are born to run and providing them with a safe hamster or running wheel gives them the opportunity to do just that.

I was 'running' in search of returning to work and normality, squeaking away on my wornout wheel.

WHAT DID I DO TO ASSIST WITH MY RECOVERY?

In total I was off work for seven and a half weeks, returning to see the doctor another two times. Each time she would talk through my symptoms, and how I was getting on. I cannot fault the doctor's surgery that we had been under. The care and attention I received were second to none.

One of the things that she suggested was that I went back to work on a phased return, reduced days and hours. And if they could not accommodate this, then I was not to go back. The medication by now had kicked in. It took a little while to settle in and I felt very drowsy to start with. My mood swings were now not so bad and at times I began to feel a little more human than I had done in previous weeks. Friends came and saw me to see how I was progressing and Pauline had been updating them on my progress.

We stayed down at the caravan for seven and a half weeks overall. I must thank the farmer who accommodated us staying in our caravan in his field for this period of time. People rallied, showed me how much they cared and wanted to support me. One of the biggest lessons that I was learning was to not fight with everyone, and giving in. My body was not fighting anymore, so why was I not listening more clearly and responding to it? Would I heed its warning if I ever found myself here again, at any point in my life?

I now had been in contact with my line manager and had arranged to go and see him at a neutral store to discuss me returning to work. We were going to be meeting in the store's café, and upon arriving, I was to discover that the Area personnel manager was also present. When I looked at them, I released that we had worked together in another store, she being my line manager and me as her training manager. I was still extremely vulnerable and when I first entered the store, the old feeling of the walls suffocating me came flooding back.

It was like I was playing a repeat movie that is shown at Christmas every year, a classic, Charles Dickens[6].'

"I am the ghost of Christmas Past. Long Past...... inquired Scrooge. No. Your past".

They were pleased to see me and commented that they had a plan in assisting me to return to work.

I listened and conveyed what the doctor had said, that I needed a phased return back to work, to which they said that they could accommodate. We then agreed a return to work date and time, that I was going to be back at work as a store manager. I understood that they were going to fully support me and ensure that I got my days off and that my new line manager would be visiting me each week in the store. They also informed me that I should have never been placed in my first store to complete my twelve-week placement and that this had been a mistake...wow! I was amazed at their honesty and transparency. They advised that I would not be returning to my previous store and would be moved to a different location and that I needed to go home and discuss this with my wife and get back to them. Otherwise, they could look for jobs back in HR. But there was no guarantee that any of these would be available.

On the one hand they were supporting me and on the other, it was that there was security in my present position, but there was no way that a new position could be created for me.

---

[6] Dickens, C. (1843) A Christmas Carol. In Prose. Being a Ghost Story of Christmas: England: Publisher. Chapman & Hall

That was how it worked.

I'm not sure what, or how I responded, but I said that I would be back in touch with them.

Of course, the doctor wanted to know what they had said to me. She was like a tiger. So, it was agreed all round, that I would be starting my new store the following week on reduced hours.

On the road to recovery

As I headed out of the house, and kissed Pauline goodbye, my heart felt heavy. The fresh air hit me as I opened the car door. On this different Monday morning, sitting in the car before I pulled off the drive, I kept repeating and saying to myself, 'this is a fresh start, a new beginning'.

As I drove the car in a different route to the one that I had previously done, my mind began to think about the new staff members I was going to meet. What had they been told about me and my situation, if anything? How would they react towards me? Would they be like the previous team that I had been working with?

I missed the junction and turning that I should have taken and got lost. I then had to turn the car around to get back onto the correct road. This was like a picture of my life, turning around and getting back onto the right road. Before long I was sat in the new store's car park. Yes, the new store's car park. Unlike the previous one where you had to park on the road, this one had one of its own. And there was only one shop next to it - a hairdressers. I smiled, thinking that there would be no more abuse from the bookies, as there was space to unload the vehicles and get the deliveries into the store.

Entering the store, I quickly found a member of staff on the till and serving and another on the shop floor, a more mature lady. They said, 'Oh, you must be Mike Abbott, our new store manager.'

They introduced themselves and we had a quick natter on the shop floor, then the team leader who was running that morning came and introduced herself. 'Would you like a cup of tea?' Well, you could have knocked me down with a feather! She took me out the back to the small kitchen, that was their break area. We chatted away and they told me about their life and the store and that they were glad to have me there. I explained that I was starting my twelve-week placement and would need to attend a sign off panel at the end of it, and hopefully get signed off and appointed.

When more staff came in, I continued to introduce myself, and found out about their lives. I could not get over the fact that I had the time and space to interact and be myself. Wow, it felt so good! My line manager and boss came to see me on that first day. Again, there was time for another tea break.

Of course, there were the CBT sessions that my doctor had booked me in for, and I had to complete the course at a nearby college facility. When the staff asked me where I was going, I just mentioned to them that I had an appointment that I needed to go to. The CBT sessions were okay, discussing how to deal with different situations and stress, and suggesting different coping mechanisms to deal with. I was also given homework, to practice on.

This was all held in a group of eight to twelve people. I felt personally that I would have preferred it more one on one, as it would have been more relevant to my life and situation, especially as we would get one person who seemed to hog the whole session. It was like this person was on some stage, performing on the X Factor, with Simon Cowell, telling the people after their audition, "Vanessa, if anyone ever asks me in my life what my nightmares look and sound like, I'm gonna refer to that." – Simon Cowell[7].

CHAPTER SUMMARY

- It had been a long seven and half weeks, from going off sick to going back to work part
- time.
- Having my Pauline make all my decisions alongside my doctor was not easy for me
- but one in which I had to swallow my pride
- At times I thought, was I ever going to get better and be able to work with people again?
- The hamster wheel
- Going back on part time hours
- A new store and a new fresh start
- The support of my new line manager and cups of tea.
- A new team that I hadn't worked with before.

---

[7] Cowell, S. 45 Most Brutal Simon Cowell Quotes (Online). Available at https://wealthygorilla.com/simon-cowell-quotes/ (Accessed: 17th January 2020)

4

Light at the End of the Tunnel

BEGINNING TO FEEL NORMAL AGAIN

As the days and weeks whisked past, and the months turned towards a new season, I was beginning to get back to how I was before I burned out and had the melt down. The store team were great to work with and getting to know the customers became part of the daily routine of asking how their families and extended families were. We had old customers who lived nearby, that we were their only family. In the bigger formats of the Company, you didn't get to hear and see this.

My boss was pleased with me and I was progressing through my Training Needs Analysis (TNA) and even managed to attend the mandatory courses that would eventually lead up to attending a sign off panel. Another huge factor in me feeling normal, was my faith in God that had kept me sane in the darkest hours.

My manager from the Group Personnel Manager came in one day unannounced and said, "I'm here to do your formal sign off as a store manager." Wow! After loads of different questions and walking me around the store, he stopped and said to me that I had passed the sign off. Getting signed off was a huge moment for me, and being appointed into that store was a major milestone in my step to becoming a store manager, working at level two and then aiming to move across formats and become a store manager, working at level 3.

It felt like over the last six months I had been walking from Land's End to John O' Groats, traversing the whole length of the island of Great Britain between two extremities, in the southwest and northeast. The traditional distance by road is eight hundred and seventy-four miles (one thousand, four hundred and seven kilometers) and takes most cyclists ten to fourteen days to complete. The traversal of coming through my melt down and getting back to work in itself was a major achievement, I could now proudly tell my friends and family that I had successfully completed my placement and was now a store manager.

A NEW JOB

Telling the staff and work collogues that I had been appointed and would not be moving anywhere else gave me great satisfaction, as I had built great working relationships and remaining in the store gave me the opportunity to plant my roots even further into the fabric of all that I and the team were trying to achieve. It was like sitting in a sofa that sucks you in and makes you never wanting to get up from it.

Still, there was a lot of work to do. As previously mentioned, the Company is a beast that continually moves forwards and never stops looking for ways to re-invent itself and offer the highest customer satisfaction index. Indeed, they had shareholders who they needed to pay back for their investment. Every year the staff had to fill in a company questionnaire, answering questions about how they felt about the company, and their working environment. Of course, the results are published and are part of the staff member's annual review. So, the company wanted the staff to answer honestly, but at the same time, I couldn't help thinking about staff members who might not say things to your face but are happy to write them down, unknowingly. Then there would be the waiting game before the results are known in the store. The data would be sent out ahead of publication, so, then the countdown would begin! And, yes, when they came out electronically, all the stores in the region could see the results - the wonder of modern technology. The results would be published and fed back, like that of a traffic light system, blue, green, amber and red.

Of course, blue meant that you had passed and exceeded everyone's expectations. Green meant that you had hit the target, amber - you were under and, well, red was not the place or result to get, as this was well below the company target and region target.

I remember looking at the e-mail with the results for our store as it landed in my inbox and as I placed the mouse over the attachment, the result opened up. The bosses said that the results were a reflection of my leadership style and management. The results for my store as their store manager came in at BLUE for the best place to work. In fact, I was later to discover, we had the best viewpoint results in the whole of my region. This certainly helped me feel normal and better. I was so proud and what little chest I had, I made sure that I pumped it out, like a huge gorilla pumping his chest for all and sundry to see in my cage of contentment.

As we were approaching Christmas and the usual staff meals were planned, we had a great meal at a local Harvester, where I made a speech and thanked the staff for all their hard work and loyalty. There are the unsung heroes within our stores and without them, the Company would not be in business and be so successful. This format that I was working in, had such a tight structure, from the staffing levels, profit upon return of investment and customer service that was second to none. Yes, I know that on the abnormal day, they had their off day, where they just didn't give great service. But on the whole, remembering that the stores were open seven days a week, and with little respite in between, they were the unsung heroes of retail.

COMING OFF ANTI-DEPRESSANT MEDICATION

I felt now that I needed to come off the medication that had been my support for the last six months. These concealed white tablets with their powers to slow down and enable me to cope with life, I had been taken rigorously throughout the third week of my burnout. But I heeded the advice of my doctor and we discussed what this was going to look like and when. The tablets I have been prescribed were the mildest form, and it was decided that I would only start taking half a tablet a day, instead of the full dosage.

I was still attending my weekly CBT sessions and others there had discussed what it was like coming off them. I was a little concerned as to how my body would react and respond, as I certainly did not want to go backwards into that dark cave, with me sat at its furthest vantage point from the entrance, curled up in ball.

I was thankful that it didn't affect my sleep pattern or cause me to not want to stop taking them, on the reduced amount. This was done with the close and very watchful eye of my GP, as they had also warned me that there could be side effects. Eventually, I came off them completely and although there had been the strange feeling at times, like my mind being fuzzy, I was so pleased and relieved to be finally separated from them, trusting that our paths would never cross again. There is so much wrong stigma and old wives' tales about telling people that you are on anti-depressants. Is it just people's pride or fear that they will judge you, for having to take them, or that you seem to be such a helpless individual who couldn't cope without the aid of your little fix me upper?

I know at first, I was reluctant to take them, but I don't think I would have been back at work and functioning without them, keeping me calm, when previously I might have flared up. I didn't mind sharing with people who I trusted, that I was taking them, but it was not something that I readily admitted. I wanted to be sure that the people I was talking with, had a genuine interest in me as a person.

I was heading into my second Christmas at the store and although the store was performing well, I began to feel that this was not the job for me. Although I felt appreciated and supported by a core team of fourteen people, I began to ponder this question over and over in my head.

GOING BACK TO WHAT I DO BEST

I also noticed that during this period of reflection, that when the pressure began to mount up on me, due to one of the shift leaders having a long period of absence, that occasionally, I began to have small and short blasted panic attacks. Nothing alarming or as dramatic as before, but they were there in the background. Was my leadership and gifting curtailed in supporting others to be at the front of the coal face, with them leading and me following?

I was now playing this game of chess in my head, playing against myself. On the one side of the table was Mike Abbott, store manager, knight in shining armour. No, this is what I'm going to do - high water or not. And on the other side of the table, this other individual, Mike Abbott, who preferred to be letting others lead and utilizing his uniqueness in supporting that and leaving them to weigh the full burden on their shoulders. It was a dichotomy that would be played out, over and over in my mind, during the coming weeks and months. It was like being at a dress rehearsal for a play, where none of the actors could get their lines right and the director repeatedly saying 'cut, cut, cut'.

I then discussed this with Pauline and wanted to get her input into what she thought. I asked her if she had seen any changes in me. She said she hadn't seen any major changes that concerned her, and that I had to make the decision and do what was right for me. But whatever I decided to do, I had her backing.

As we headed towards another Christmas and the month of December approached, I had an outburst on the shop floor when my line manager was visiting. I can't quite remember the full details, but I do recall saying that this job isn't for me anymore and I wanted to go back to being a personnel manager in another format. Upon reflection, it was not the best place to be carrying on this type of conversation, in front of passing customers and staff who were working nearby.

We then withdrew to an office and I told him that I wanted the Area personnel manager to start looking for an alternative role for me. Of course, none of the staff knew what I had, or was planning to do. I had now reached the point where I was making my own decisions.

This time, I also wanted to leave on my terms and not on some fellow Store Director's badly timed preference, holding me as his puppet, controlling my strings and pulling them in the direction they had decided was best for my life and career. So, in the following January, I had found and been offered a job back in another format, as a Personnel Manager. It was sad saying goodbye to the staff and work colleagues, but it was time to be going back to what I knew how to do best. I walked out of the store on that final day, with my head held high.

Chapter Summary

- The satisfaction of beginning to feel like a normal human being again.
- My mind had not deserted me, but had been buried in the depths of my despair and torment.
- I had finally passed my sign off for store manager in the smaller formats.
- The joy of telling my friends and family that I had succeeded at long last.
- That amazing blue staff questionnaire and result, which was the best in my region.
- Being able to thank the staff personally at the Christmas meal, was so important to me.

- Telling my line manager that it was time for me to return to what I was best at
- Leaving the store with my head held high.

5

Making Crucial Decisions

THE DANGER OF DOING WHAT OTHER PEOPLE THINK IS BEST FOR YOU

As I moved back into personnel and retuned to being part of a leadership team, where I was now not the sole person in charge of the store, in other words the buck didn't stop with me, it made me realise how important it is not living your life by doing what others say is the best way for you.

Taking advice and following someone else's well-meaning suggestions and their experience can lead one to not utilize and think for ones-self. Then there is within society the peer pressure that you also have to attain and be at a certain vantage point at this time in your life. This I found, was typically true of when I was at school, where you had to sit a test. The system back then said that if you were not at this level, then this is where you were going to stay throughout your school years. For me, was the danger of then being classed as a remedial pupil who was stitched up with this label which was applied to me. I was never seen as someone with the potential to move upwards and out of this stigma, so when I left school with no qualifications, I was now having to face a world in which that moving upwards and beyond was going to be difficult.

Then upon entering the crazy word of training to be a chef, emphasized it even more. Again, there was the top stream and you then fitted in where they thought was best. This is how you do it and, no, you can't think for yourself – this was the general attitude. I appreciate that if you want to pass an exam and be trained up to work at the recognized level, you have to work through the required training. But what if people don't get it as fast as you would like them to? I know I'm talking about some over forty years ago and the education system has come a long way since. We accommodate people with different learning styles today, but for me, putting people in a box and saying this is the best way for you, is so dangerous, and can lead to not fulfilling the potential that has been placed in you from birth.

George King Thompson, would agree entirely with this. In

an article, by Hannah[8] stated that "Prison isn't much of a stretch once you've knocked off the Shard". It tells the story of George King Thompson, who climbed the Shard without any ropes or support. Thompson claimed that he leant more behind bars than at his forty-thousand pounds a year private school. The article goes on to state, "He is certain life should be spent following what you are passionate about -regardless of the risk of death or prison".

I agree with George, that you should be able to follow your passions, minus climbing the Shard without any ropes! This I found to be so true within my own organization, that when you had that yearly career discussion, or where the next position within the company would be suitable, it inevitably was mostly done with what they thought was best and for them to fulfill the supply chain. I'm not saying that they didn't want you to think, but it was really challenging if you decided no, this is not what I want to do.

I remember a person joining my first store, who had been brought in to set up a new department, I won't say which one it was, as I want to respect their privacy. However, I clearly remember that this person, who was on the top team within the store management, had fresh ideas of how he was going to run the department. He clashed with the store manager who just couldn't see this new way of doing things. It was like they were old cowboys, ready to gun fight at the O.K. Corral. But the new person was not going to budge and it was very interesting watching from the 'salon bar'!

Having gone through my burnout, I was determined upon

---

[8] Hannah, E., (2020). Prison isn't much of a stretch once you've knocked off the Shard. The Sunday Times.

returning to the role of Personnel, that when I sat down with people who were asking for my advice on what was best for them, I would say, well, have a think about this and go away and think what's best for you. I also believe that the danger of sheep-dipping everyone with the same brush is dangerous and can lead individuals to dysfunction.

I recollect having discussions with some of our students who worked part-time in the store, who were gaining some extra money whilst working their way through college and university. Some of whom would tell me, from certain ethnic populations, that it was expected of them to become a doctor or lawyer and woe betide them if they rebelled. I felt sorry for them.

How do you know what's right for you?

For me, I think it is important to go away and not make rash and impulsive decisions, which later I then regret making. I have certainly made every mistake that you can think of, like buying a motor bike once, that was too powerful for me, and I had done no forward planning or thinking of how I was going to pass my test and learn to ride this. Just one of Mike Abbott's crazy ideas. Throughout my life I have been very thankful for those people who have been there at the right time - people who I respected and valued their input into my life.

Uniqueness of your journey (and don't lose sight of who you are)

Then, there is enjoying the uniqueness of being yourself. You see, as I had gone through burnout, I had lost being me. It somehow got buried in the sea of despair and had been replaced with being depressed and not being able face life again. It is a terrible thing to lose one's identity, and finding it was part of the recovery process that I went through - rebuilding your self-esteem and not losing sight of who you are. It was like I was back on the range trying to hit the target and missing, because I needed to adjust the weapon, as it must point naturally at the target without undue physical effort. For me, this was doing a job that I was not meant to do and so placing my life under undue pressure.

What were the uniqueness and qualities that made Mike Abbott and shaped his journey of the person he has become today? I think the following captured them:

- Committed
- Loyal
- Trustworthy
- Hard working
- Team player
- Sense of humour
- Teachable

If you are struggling with your own identity, then can I encourage you to sit down with a piece of paper and simply write down the things that you believe that you are good at, enjoy doing and seeing if there is a pattern? Or even ask a family member that you trust, to give you honest feedback and then compare what they say to what you have written. Like our DNA, we are all unique, and it is vitally important to never forget this.

Lessons learnt and what I had to implement

Having now been at work for some months in the role of Personnel, and having a life outside work, what were the lessons I had to implement or remind myself of on a daily basis? I pose this question as there were times it was as if I found myself with two heads, being portrayed as a double-headed llama, like something out of the film, *Doctor Dolittle*[9], and in fact, was walking around the store with part of it in Store Manager Mode, and the other, Personnel Manager.

It took me a while to adjust and others would comment that it felt like there were two store managers telling them what to do! It was not helpful, and I wish I could have gone through a car wash and come out the other side, having lost my 'store manager head', and instead now walking entirely with a fully polished mat wax 'new head'. It is said that it takes thirty days to learn a new habit and behavior; some would say they couldn't wait for my thirty days to be up!

Chapter Summary

- Losing one head and focusing on the right one
- Enjoy being yourself and living the best version of you.
- Education wrongly classifies that we should be at this vantage point by a certain age.
- Follow your passions as long as you don't climb the Shard without any ropes!

---

[9] Doctor Dolittle (1967) Directed by Richard Fleischer (Film). Los Angeles: 20th Century Fox

- Being allowed to bring your fresh perspective to your work and not having to gun fight at the O.K. Corral every day.
- Not making rash decisions and taking your time to think them through.
- What qualities do you have? Write them down and enjoy using them.
- If you change jobs, remember what your new role is and isn't! Life is easier with one head.

6

Not neglecting other areas of your life.

BEING DRIVEN IS OKAY, BUT NOT WHEN IT'S ALL CONSUMING

There is always a right balance in getting to one's pre-determined, desired, career aspirations, but then this can become all-consuming. I was so focused and driven, without any safety car to keep me from hurting myself. Yes, you do need to have the get up and go, so that when things are tough you get back up again and dust yourself down, and go again. But as I have learnt in later life, goals need to be SMART (Specific, Measurable, Achievable, Realistic, and Timely). Therefore, a SMART goal incorporates all of these criteria to help focus your efforts and increase the chances of achieving that goal.

But mine were not SMART, in fact they were more like the following:

ACDC (All consuming, Dangerous, totally career minded)

Another definition that I liked is: "Someone who is driven is so determined to achieve something or be success-

Not neglecting other areas of your life.

ful that all of their behavior is directed towards this aim".

You see, my behaviors and driving aims were focused so badly on wanting to become a Group Personnel Manager, work level three within the Company - this was my dream. I was an Extreme Dodgems (banger racing rally car) called Mike Abbott, whose compulsion, was eat, sleep, work, eat, sleep, and work. I was blinkered to the outside world and domain that this all new overshadowing world was all that I could see in front of me.

Yes, I know it's important to have goals, but in getting there I had risked my own life and sanity. The demands that I had placed on my body were frightening. Was it worth it, to be told by your doctor that you were close to having a nervous breakdown and that your life would never be the same? *Mike, your body has given you a warning that you need and never be in this place ever again!*

But it is easy to get caught up in the rat race of life. Especially when you think that what you are committing to will give you a better quality of life for your family, like more money, better house and car. This is something that I had seen others do and had been successful with their careers. But what I didn't often see, was the toll that it had placed on them personally and their families.

They never fully disclosed in the conversations with me what was occurring in their private lives. Everything looked rosy on the surface, but what was really happening in their own gardens of life?

As my wife would have told you, if you had the opportunity

to speak with her, you would have seen and heard from her perspective about living with this all-consuming man, called Mike Abbott. Was my level of drive also having an effect on the way I treated people, trying to be someone that I clearly was not? I recall having a member of staff who was stuck in his ways, and in the format that I worked in you had to be able to do everything, serve on the till, and then fill the store once the deliveries had arrived. It was go, go, go. So, as the Store Manager, one day I took him outside and gave him a roasting, at the side of the car park. This was no political correctness, or in an office chat, it was no holds barred. I told him if he didn't improve or start pulling his weight, then I would be getting rid of him by any means possible, as he was not going to stop me in my drive and ambition to succeed.

This was not the way I had treated people throughout my career and certainly not up to the point of being in placement as a store manager, in the smaller format. It was like I had lost my logical and rational side of my head. Where had the previous Mike Abbott gone, my head was asking. Can you please bring him back ASAP!

And then if something didn't arrive that we needed in store, the stress and anger that got hold of me, when shouting and bawling at people down the phone would be heard from the office onto the shop floor. If depot managers, or services that the store should have got, like the daily cleaner had not turned up, I would then throw out the area manager when he arrived to do his weekly audit and tell him to sort it, or not bother coming back! My boss, phoned me after this incident and asked me what was going on.

Not neglecting other areas of your life.

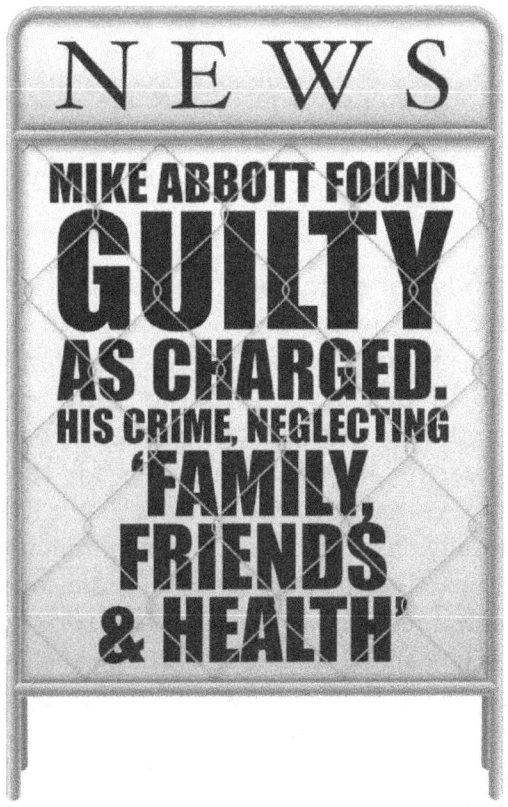

NEGLECTING MY SPACE

In a courtroom scenario being played out, I was guilty as charged. "Mike Abbott, you are responsible for doing something illegal that you have been **accused** of in court: He was found guilty **as charged** and fairly tried, and therefore justice was served. His crime - neglecting family, friends, health and recreational activities. Mike Abbott is now awaiting sentencing. The judge has warned him that he is facing a custodial sentence!"

By putting others and my job before me. It was not something that I thought about, or had the time or inkling to make space for. But sitting in a jail cell would have helped me see the errors of my way.

I had certainly not given Pauline the attention that she so rightly deserved, she was a retail widower. The other woman in my life and in our relationship was the Company, which had consumed all my energy. And when I did return home, I was so tired and worn out, that all I wanted to do was sleep. I remember going on holiday and always for the first three days, I was nonexistent, as I was so tired, that it took me three days to eventually feel like doing anything, much to Pauline's frustration. Then the times over the Christmas period that I would not get home until around seven-thirty at night or later on Christmas Eve and would walk through the door looking like a zombie in a horror movie. The missed parties and functions over the years all mounted up, as I was working weekends, bank holidays, days into lates, and covered the shortage of shifts, due to the wage restraints.

The additional hours of commuting to work weren't allowing me time and space to recharge my batteries. Not only was I getting stuck in traffic, and if you then left a bit later and got jammed in the traffic of the day, would be another two hours easily on top of your journey - all this just to land in my stores as a Multi-site personnel manager, and start working. I wasn't like the current hybrid cars on the road today, that by having an engine which can switch from electric, to petrol - no it was me running on me, empty.

I never did any hobbies or had time to give my brain a rest

Not neglecting other areas of your life.

---

from the constant and never-ending world of people. Dealing with people all day is very demanding, as you are often listening to some really unbelievable things they are telling you. You can't wander off, and your concentration levels must be at their best.

One day I was in one of my stores, organizing the staff Christmas lunch, setting up the tables and running around like a lunatic. At the same time, in one of my other stores, where I was the multi-site Personnel manager, I was having to deal with the pension for a terminally ill member of staff. I had been liaising with this family for weeks and weeks, as this employee wanted to receive their final salary pension and exercise their right to pay it out to their family before they died. I had to phone the doctor at the hospice they were in, as we had a very short window in order to get this through, otherwise they would have lost thousands of pounds, and I was responsible.

The call came through on my mobile as I was being jolly and trying to cheer up the staff. I had to excuse myself and go into an office and take the call. The doctor confirmed the information that I needed, and went through their life expectancy, and what was going to occur in their final hours. Well, I was in bits, crying and trying to hold my emotions together, so I could then phone the pensions department immediately as well as get the doctor at the hospice to fax over a copy to me and then send it on to pensions.

Of course, the staff at my present store were wondering where I had got to. Again, I just was on auto pilot and went straight back in, without giving myself time and space to get back to being normal, or just being able to get out of the store and go for a walk.

The mobile phone that allows people to get hold of you twenty-four seven, seven days a week did not help, and I was constantly getting into e-mails. I was completely sold out to my life within the Company. My relationships with my close friends suffered as a result. There was the occasional phone call, but arranging to see them to catch up was difficult. I was not aware of this and was blinded, or just didn't give myself the time and space to see it.

RE-BUILDING MY WORK LIFE BALANCE (SAFE-GUARDS)

It was through a set of circumstances and changes within my role of personnel that got me re-building my work life balance. I was asked again by my current Group Personnel Manager to go and work in two different stores. At this point, my contracted hours were supposed to be thirty-six and a half hours a week. As previously mentioned, I did way beyond this and more.

So, one of the new stores that I would be working in for two days a week, was accessible by train, and by Pauline taking me to our local station, the train would now be taking the strain. It was such a fresh experience to be sitting with other people, who didn't work in retail. I often had conversations with so many interesting people - finding out about their industries that they worked in, was therapeutic. Yes, people did talk to me. Maybe it was the sticker on my forehead that said please be kind to this individual, he's not often let out into the outside world.

I knew people would say, Mike you've lost it. But I really

Not neglecting other areas of your life.

---

looked forward to those days when I could be in another world, other than retail; I know it sounds strange. Yes, there were the cancellations and delayed service, but I was able to sit back and read a book on the journey to the station. Looking out of the window and seeing the beautiful countryside as I passed it by, began to awaken me to the fact that there was life outside. Also, I would often hear people say what they were going to do at the week-ends.

Then, there was the short distance to walk to the store; getting some exercise would be doing me some good. Another thing I had to be mindful of was that what time I would be leaving work in order to get home. It was not something that I just put my head down once at work – no! I had to make a conscious decision of what time the train would be taking me home in the evening. It made me explain to the store manager and the management team that I was here until this time and if they wanted to discuss anything with me, then this was the window of opportunity.

And again, with a new structure change, it was decided that I did not have to be part of the Rota when opening and closing the stores. So that part of my role was now Monday to Friday. Well, I thought I had gone to heaven. What I was going to do with two days off together, in the first time in my working life at the Company?

I could plan in advance when we would go and see my family at the week-ends, or have friends over for a meal. It took time to re-adjust to having the space to think and recharge my batteries. I then put some safeguards in my time off. These included switching the phone off and having to discipline myself that I didn't need to answer every call, and by leaving a voice mail message when I was now on holiday, and the date and time I would return. This helped me enormously. I was now beginning to get a work life balance. Friends commented that I looked better and Pauline said I was more relaxed and not so stressed out.

Here are some of the other safeguards that I found helpful and enabled me to get more of a work life balance:

- Accepting that not everything is life-threating, there are other people who can deal with that situation
- Training other people up to do my job
- Better time management
- Saying no
- Getting some fresh air
- Talking to others outside of retail
- Setting boundaries
- Having my breaks

> *Has my belly chuckled with laughter today?*
>
> Mike Abbott

BEING ABLE TO LAUGH AGAIN!

I had often had days and weeks where I had forgotten how to laugh again, and especially at myself. As the great Charlie

Chaplin[10] said: "A day without laughter is a day wasted". How many days had I wasted by not laughing? Being in burn out and depressed and not being able to face the world is a dark place. But in all that had happened over the weeks and months, it had evaporated away into thin air.

Marilyn Monroe[11] put it this way, "Nothing lasts forever, so live it up, drink it down, laugh it off, avoid the drama, take chances, and never have regrets. Because at one point everything you did was exactly what you wanted".

They say laughter is the best medicine and I have a great sense of humor, a little dry, which comes from my father who has the fastest one-liners that I knew. My experience of being in the Army band developed it even further. But how was I going to rediscover it and allow it to come out again? Spending time with my friends helped re- kindle it into action and brought it back to life. One of my close friends, Roger, just by being with him did me good; he is great company to be with, and a little bonkers.

Sitting down with Pauline and watching a funny TV program also helped, or a good film. One of our favorites is *See Spot Run*[12], a Canadian-American comedy film about a mailman who takes in a stray bull mastiff, the titular Spot,

---

[10] Chaplin, C. (2001) (Online). Available at https://www.brainyquote.com/quotes/charlie_chaplin_108932/ (Accessed 17th January 2020)

[11] Monroe, M. Marilyn Monroe Nothing Last Forever Quotes (Online) Available at (https://www.inspirationboost.com/marilyn-monroe-nothing-last-forever-quotes/ (Accessed 17th January 2020)

[12] See Spot Run (2001) Directed by John Whitesell (Film). Canada: Warner Bros. Pictures

only to learn that he is a trained FBI agent. It's a kid's film, but it does you well, if you like that sort of thing.

Little by little, I began to find myself laughing often at little things that caught me by surprise, and out would come a chuckle. Unfortunately, I have inherited my mother's laugh; once it is fully loaded and in full flight, it completely takes over - a great tonic! It affects everyone and is so infectious, that it leaves you with no choice but to join in, or stare at me in scorn. I realized that being able to laugh was what I needed.

Chapter Summary

- Being driven and having career ambition is okay, as long as it is not all encompassing.
- So important to get the right balance in all areas of your life.
- Need the safety car to keep you from derailing.
- Having SMART goals and not ACDC ones.
- Ensuring that you don't lose sight of all the other areas within your life.
- Listening to your body.
- Having real conversation with people and finding out what their real world is like.
- Is your ladder facing the right wall for your life?
- Don't become someone that you're not.
- Live by your core values.
- Making time and space for yourself.
- Not neglecting your family and friends
- Having hobbies.
- Laughter is so important.
- Turning off the phone.

Not neglecting other areas of your life.

- Seeing that there is an outside window.
- Setting boundaries and safeguards.

7

How to identify when you are near burnout...what the signs are!

MY SYMPTOMS AND WARNING SIGNS

Well, there were many warning signs over the days and months leading up to me completely having a full breakdown, relating to burnout, which I completely ignored. If I could have been a bystander observing myself traveling back in time as a time traveler, before the events took place, and stepping out of the usage of an imaginary science fiction time machine, I would have seen the major warning signs being my behavior patterns.

I'm not proud of any of them; it wasn't like I was suddenly aware of them. And they weren't all there at the same time. I was exceptionally impatient, I couldn't' wait – no, it had to be done now. "Come on, get a move on!" was my cry of the day. And I wouldn't listen. Pauline would be saying to me time and again, you can't carry on, (way before that day of sitting on the bed, when my body said, 'He ain't listening to us either. I don't know what fat chance you have of getting through to his think skin'). When we did have dinner, inevitably, the conver-

How to identify when you are near burnout...what the signs are!

sation would turn to the subject matter in hand, my health. I would cut Pauline down and say, you know what I signed up to, and more importantly, you agreed to support me in the process of getting signed off and appointed as store manager.

I was being totally impartial and one-sided towards Pauline in my defense and counter argument.

I had to carry on no matter what, as in the words of Winston Churchill[13], "It's not enough that we do our best; sometimes we have to do what's required." And that's what I was doing. That's what was required.

Additionally, I was obsessed with not letting people down, like attending my nephew James' birthday party in London, which I mentioned in an earlier chapter. No, I simply wouldn't have it. There were staff in the store who could let me down and not turn up for whatever reason for their shifts. But not Mike Abbott, no, no no. He kept going and going and going.

The other symptoms that I had included a very short fuse, which made me lose my cool quickly, like an agitated dog on a lead, baring its razor-sharp teeth, ready to pounce on you at any moment as you walked past. I have listed other symptoms below:

- Lack of sleep
- Sweating
- Exhausted all the time

---

[13] Churchill, W. (2015) Forbes Quotes Thoughts On The Business Of Life. Available at https://www.forbes.com/quotes/10319/ (Accessed 17th January 2020)

- Feeling cynical towards my work
- Demands of my job were overwhelming
- Took it out on Pauline, not physically

EFFECTS ON MY FAMILY

They say that alcoholics and drug users are not concerned about the effect it has on them and their families, as long as they are getting their drink or a fix. Burnout to me can be classed alongside alcohol and drug disease. Even the World Health Authority has classed burnout as a disease, and it will be recognized as such in 2022[14]. This disease as I shall call it, had major effects on my beautiful wife Pauline. I caused her undue stress and tears, especially when I would phone up without any warning, having one of my many panic attacks at any point throughout the day or night. I would just upload on her, like someone vomiting up their entire insides and leaving the other person to clear it up, the remains dumped in their laps. The mental pressure I also put her through, I really don't know how she put up with it all and still remained married to me. It must have been hell for her, living with Mike Abbott.

Other members of my family also suffered. My parents, seeing me at James' twenty-first birthday party - what must have been going through their minds, and them feeling so hopeless. As I left and was going back to work the following week, I could see it now, looking back, on the strains upon their faces as we left - their cries of "please take care of

---

[14] Daily Mail (2020) (Online). Available at https://www.dailymail.co.uk/health/article-7076089/Burn-officially-recognized-disease-World-Health-Organization.html/ (Accessed 17 th January 2020)

yourself", and worrying frowns. The phone calls that followed and the tone of their voices on the other end of the line were evidence that they were really concerned, especially when Pauline had to phone them up and tell them what happened on that black day. Not being privy to what had been said, it cannot have been easy for Pauline as she relayed the bad news!

TOLL ON MY HEALTH AND WELL-BEING

There was a huge toll placed upon my health and well-being, I could have had a heart attack and died, and that would have been it. I was putting so much strain and pressure on my heart, and mind. I'm surprised that it didn't conk out sooner, as I certainly wasn't listening to it. When eventually I did stop, it needed so much sleep to help it to recover (more of which I will discuss in the next chapter). My wellbeing was the last item, on my personalised shopping list, hidden beneath the layers of so many other things:

- Work
- Career & ambition
- Pleasing other people
- Not saying no

My body was like a fish, flapping around on dry land, crying and longing for someone to return (me) to the ocean. I was so desperate and needed a fresh supply of oxygen to breathe again. The fumes I had been consuming on a daily basis were toxic and harmful to my whole system. This had been months of abuse.

Additionally, like the fish that takes its water in its mouth and passes it through its gills, I was not eating healthily. What was passing through my mouth into my gills was unhealthy, eating on the go, chewing as I moved towards another delivery, slurping a cup of tea with two to three sugars! If my car needs a service or has its annual MOT completion, then without hesitation it is booked in, yes, it is a legal requirement. I, on the other hand was running without an up to date MOT! No breaks and no rest periods, with worn out tyres.

Some symptoms have remained

There is the odd occasion that some of my past symptoms flare up. I'm not talking about the panic attacks, or melting down, but sometimes I can be very impatient with Pauline and a bit snappy, especially when we have to leave the house by a certain time. I detest being late, and since my burnout, this has been highlighted even more. It's like I'm so obsessed that I run around, saying, "Come on, let's get moving!" I also feel compelled to plan the departure time well in advance, or else I can get stressed out easily. It is something that I'm aware of, and often get reminded about by Pauline!

Chapter Summary

- Ignoring my body's warning signs
- Obsessed with not letting people down
- Not getting the required sleep
- Not eating healthy
- Eating on the go
- No breaks to re-charge my batteries
- Placing my wellbeing last on my personalised shopping list

How to identify when you are near burnout...what the signs are!

- Burnout is a disease as recognised by the World Health Authority in 2022[15]
- The dangers and consequences of not listening, you reap what you sow.

---

[15] Daily Mail (2020) (Online). Available at https://www.dailymail.co.uk/health/article-7076089/Burn-officially-recognized-disease-World-Health-Organization.html/ (Accessed 17 th January 2020)

8

Tools to get back up!

Please see the enclosed table (Table 1) for my list of tools, that I used to get back up, and some suggested actions to follow:

Table 1. Tools to get back up

Tools	What I did	Action
Doctors/input	I don't know what your relationship is like with your local GP surgery, but this was such a necessary aid in me getting back up	If you haven't registered with your local GP, I would suggest that you do, especially if you are burnt out and need their assistance.
Family and Friends	Chilling out with my wife and friends, was something that helped me enormously.	When was the last time you chilled with your friends?
Re-energize the mind	Having those different conversations on the	Is all your conversation about work?

	train stimulated my mind away from retail.	
Sleep	It was so important to me, I just didn't realise how much my body needed it – seven and a half hours	Take a note of your sleep patterns and see if you are getting enough for you
Cognitive Behavioral Therapy (CBT)	CBT, showed me how to use different techniques in changing the way that I had been thinking and behaving.	Find out about CBT and do some research.
Breaks	Just sitting down and taking the weight off my feet, and having that break at work gave my mind a chance to regroup. Having a day off with no work and that a lie in was bliss.	Are you having your breaks and days off?
Laughter	It was so good to laugh, and enjoy watching a movie that made me chuckle.	Do something that makes you laugh. Watch comedy or do those things that bring a smile to your face.
Getting outside	Just that short walk from the station to work - it was great being outdoors,	When was the last time you got some fresh air?

	when my world of work was inside.	Go for a walk in the park or forests.
Personal Space	Safeguarding my personal space became so important to me. Re-setting parameters, upon which I could have time to think and reflect, and not allowing it to be breached, gave me new breathing space.	Who dictates your personal space? Take time to review what you are allowing in. Take stock of your life again.
Different transportation to work	Not driving to work and letting the train take the strain, enabled me to do other things, like reading and chatting to other passengers.	See if there is a different mode of transport to get to work.

There is another great tool, see (Table 2), which I currently do, which centres around my food, exercise and health, and my feelings towards. Again, the action I will take are under each heading:

Table 2:

My approaches to...		
FOOD	**EXERCISE**	**HEALTH**
What transpires daily/weekly: - Eat junk food - Consume on the go - Having to reheat it in the microwave - Don't plan my meals. - Too many sugars in my tea	**What transpires daily/weekly:** - None apart from unloading lorries and filling shelves	**What transpires daily/weekly:** - Don't have time to review my health and wellbeing. - Not aware of the warning signs my body is giving me.
My Goals: Watch what I eat and cut out the biscuits and chocolates	**My Goals:** Find time to go for a walk with the dogs	**My Goals:** Speak to my doctor about my health and have a MOT.
My Action Plan: Select a day to take a packed lunch to work	**My Action Plan:** Get a day off	**My Action Plan:** Phone GP surgery

A certain activity I will do:	A certain activity I will do:	A certain activity I will do:
Join a slimming group and plan my meals	Have a day off and go for a walk with the dogs	Book a date to see my GP.

CHAPTER SUMMARY

- The importance of finding tools that will enable you to re- gain your life
- There may be others that you think are better suited for you personally, but try the above exercises (Table 1) and (Table 2) and see what happens.

9

Making sure you get the right mentor

My experience of working with different mentors (good & ugly)

You may well be asking what a chapter on mentorship and finding the right one, is doing in a book about burnout and the pathway to recovery. However, I think the lack of a mentor, was one of the reasons I got burnt out. The Collins Shorter Dictionary and Thesaurus16 defines the work 'mentor', as the following:

- Advisor
- Coach
- Counsellor
- Guide
- Guru
- Instructor
- Teacher
- Tutor

---

[16] Mentor (1991). In: Collins Shorter Dictionary and Thesaurus. St Helens, page 469.

Alternatively, it can mean the guidance provided by a mentor, especially an experienced person in a company or educational institution, as seen in the examples of use below:

"He is revered by his employees for his mentorship and problem-solving qualities."

"A period of time during which a person receives guidance from a mentor."

"A two-year mentorship with an entrepreneur in a tech start-up".

I have experienced the good, the bad and the ugly, like in the film, *Spaghetti Western*[17], during my working lifetime.

> *A true mentor inspires you to take action, so that you fulfil your destiny*
>
> Mike Abbott

---

[17] The Good, the Bad and the Ugly (1966) Directed by Sergio Leone (Film). Italy: United Artists

GOOD MENTOR EXPERIENCE

I remember my first ever business mentor/advisor, called Steve. He was someone who I admired, and had been extremely successful; he was a Sales Director for a company. As well as working for his current company, he had also worked in other companies and gained a lot of experience and insights, to how to succeed in life.

I reached out to him for some career advice and he suggested that we meet at a local pub, one evening to catch up. What I noticed about his approach, was when we sat down to have a drink and a chat, he was totally focused on me, listening and thinking about what I was saying to him. He had taken time out of his busy schedule to spend quality time with Mike Abbott. He was not puffed up or had a big ego – no, he was here to help and wanted me to tell my story, of how I had arrived at this moment in my working life. He knew a little about me, as our paths had crossed at church. But that was about it, really.

As I began to share with him, and the conversation flowed back and forth, he made suggestions and backed them up with examples of what he had done. There was no, 'this is what you have got to get done and report back to me'. I did jot down in a note book, some of his suggestions and we agreed to meet the following month.

When the evening had finished, I thanked him for his time, and as I went home, I was so inspired by him, it was a pleasure being in his company. Wow! It made me spring to action with my next steps and plan of books I was going to read. As a result of working with Steve for a short period of time, one of his suggestions was gaining a professional qualification in my chosen field, and to see how I could go about doing this, such as getting funding, as well as other related matters. This had been based on me leaving school with no formal qualifications. So, many years later, I gained my MSc in Human Resources Development. I would not have this industry-recognised degree without his input and mentorship in my life.

BAD MENTOR EXPERIENCE

Unfortunately, I had been spoilt by my first ever mentor, and the next person who became my mentor, was going to have to live up to his bench mark and high standards. It was many, many years later that my line manager suggested that I work with this mentor and to see if I could arrange to meet them. I duly phoned this person up and spoke with their secretary about securing an appointment. She knew nothing about why I was calling and had not been kept in the loop by her boss, as my line manger did have a conversation with this person in question. Great. However, I pushed through and explained what it was about. She eventually looked in their diary and we made an appointment for when the person would be in my area.

The due date arrived and I had left my current place of work in good time, to go and drive the distance, to meet at this mutually agreed convenient store. The appointed time arrived and there was no show of this person. So, I was left there wondering what was going on and what to do. I tried calling him on his mobile phone and it went straight to voice mail. I then tried calling his secretary to see if he had an emergency to deal with, and that the plan was still to arrive to see me. "Yes," she informed me. "He was still on route." He eventually arrived some two hours later for our meeting, and when we did sit down, his mind was elsewhere, totally not focused on me. It was a complete waste of my time and effort to get there. Additionally, he had his agenda, and focus on how my career should progress. Come back Steve, please! This arrangement never worked out and I regretted my boss' suggestion. It was unwanted stress that I just didn't need.

MY VIEWS ON FINDING THE RIGHT MENTOR

Over the years, I have come to the realisation that mentorship is built out of relationships. For it to work in my life, it has to be this or nothing else. Yes, I know that there are people who I might go and see about a subject matter to gain their insights, or attend a talk that they are giving. But to sit down with someone as a potential mentor, I have got to know that they are genuinely interested in helping and guiding me forward and not backward. This is non-negotiable and I won't budge from this stand point. Life is fragile and time is a limited resource that cannot be wasted. I do not have another day to waste - my time is like precious gold. When deciding to move to a new bank, for example, I certainly want to know about their overall performance and track record. It takes time on my part to decide if I'm moving or not. Likewise, it takes time and commitment on each part of the mentor /mentee relationship for it to work. I also think that it is a good idea to go and have a coffee with the person in mind, if that is feasible, to find out if you are going to be able to work with them. I've learnt the hard way and don't want to repeat the same mistakes.

Here are some points to consider in establishing such a relationship:

- Will the mentor follow up on what they say they're going to do?
- Is the suggested mentor that you have been assigned to work with, your idea or the company's?
- Do they have a good track record of working with previous mentees?
- Is it part of their job description and objectives, in which they have to meet their KPIs and receive their annual bonus?
- Have either of you had the necessary training to undergo this, as you don't want to be another sheep having to be dipped, like the rest of the herded mentees, going nowhere and stuck in your pen!

Like I said previously, I've seen the good the bad the ugly in the area of mentorship

THE WORLD NEEDS MENTORS

I have had the privilege of traveling to some amazing places outside the United Kingdom, seeing the different continents and islands of this world. One of the greatest things that I have witnessed is, when people explain that they are where they are, because of another person who has helped them on their personal journey. They may not have used the word, 'mentor', but it certainly falls under that category described in the Collins Shorter dictionary and thesaurus[18].

---

[18] Mentor (1991). In: Collins Shorter Dictionary and Thesaurus. St Helens, page 469.

In all walks of life, from business to sports and beyond, here is list of people who have been mentors to others and they have then impacted their worlds: Dutta[19]

- Warren Buffet mentor to Michael Lee-Chin (Chairman of National Commercial Bank in Jamaica)
- Steve Jobs to Marc Benioff.
- Larry Page mentor to Marissa Mayer (CEO Yahoo)
- Audrey Hepburn mentor to Elizabeth Taylor
- Mel Gibson mentor to Heath Ledger
- Joseph Papp mentor to Meryl Streep
- Denzel Washington mentored by Sidney Poitier
- George Mason mentor to Thomas Jefferson (3rd President of the US)
- Gopal Krishna Gokhale mentor to Mahatma Gandhi
- Dadabhai Naoroji mentor to Mahatma Gandhi
- Mahatma Gandhi mentor to Dr. Martin Luther King, Jr.
- Mahatma Gandhi mentor to Nelson Mandela
- Vikram Sarabhai mentor to APJ Abdul Kalam
- Dr. Martin Luther King, Jr. mentor to Jesse Jackson and John Lewis
- Fidel Castro (President of Cuba) mentor to Hugo Chavez (President of Venezuela)
- Michelle Robinson (lawyer) mentor to Barack Obama
- Annie Besant (English social reformer and theosophist) mentor to Jiddu Krishnamurti (Indian reli-

---

[19] Dutta, A. (2014) (Online). Available at https://www.quora.com/What-are-some-examples-of-great-mentors-in-the-history-of-the-world/ (Accessed 17th January 2020)

gious figure)
- Ralph Waldo Emerson mentor to Henry David Thoreau
- Christian Dior mentor to Yves Saint Laurent
- Sachin Tendulkar mentor to Virender Sehwag
- Boris Becker is a mentor to Novak Djokovic

BEING A MENTOR TO OTHERS (MY NON-NEGOTIABLE)

When individuals or colleagues have asked me to be their mentor, of course I do count it a great honor and privilege that someone wants me to assist them. But my dark sense of humour that lies beneath the surface, ponders and thinks ...... you must be mad! Totally bonkers!

But, what sort of mentor are you looking for? This is a great starting point. And this always takes me back to the different experiences of mentorship that I went through. Here are a few questions that I ask myself before committing to saying yes:

- Do I have the time and commitment that they so richly deserve?
- Am I the best person and fit for what they are requiring?
- How long for? Is this short term and for how many weeks?
- What support will they need in between our sessions?
- How many face to face meetings or telephone conversations?
- Follow up on what they saying they're going to

commit to do, before the next meeting.
- It's their meeting, so shut up and remember, your point of view or opinion is not why they are here.

CHAPTER SUMMARY

- Finding and working with the right mentor will enable you to reach you potential.
- Listening is a key skill in being a mentor.
- Following up on your commitments is essential in the mentor/mentee relationship.
- Doing what it says on the tin is vital to not losing credibility.
- Remember the Spaghetti Western philosophy.
- If it's not working, stop.
- Who's deciding on why you should work with this person as your mentor?
- Who's going to be the next mentor to the next Warren Buffet?

10

Hope for your Future

MY LIFE NOW COMPARED TO WHAT IT WAS

My life is completely different to what it was like back then, when I got burnt out. I no longer work for the Company or in the world of retail. After a management re-structure by the company, my position became no longer required. And after several consultations, I opted for redundancy.

After being with the company for twenty years and saying my goodbyes, it was time to head out the door and into a new world.

I'm so glad that I did, as I was able to take all that I had learnt and experienced, and place it into my own company, 'mikehabbott.com'. I certainly discovered a lot about working for myself in those first few months, and from my initial errors that I made. I no longer had the vast mechanism of a large corporation behind me – no, the buck stopped with me, and this was another huge learning curve for me.

As well as offering my Human Resources services to small and medium-sized enterprises (SMEs), in 2017, I completed my Postgraduate Certificate in Business and Personnel Coaching, with the University of Chester, which gave me the opportunity to expand my business in the world of coaching. Having personally experienced burnout and its impact within my own life, and seeing the devasting effects it once had, I was now able to help my clients move forward within their own lives if they were suffering from burnout. Additionally, what I also love about coaching is, it is always about focusing on the future and not the past.

One of the coaching model by Egan's (The Skilled- Helper[20]) can be an effective coaching tool, which enables the person in front of you to tell you their story and helps the client change perspective, breaking down limiting beliefs. The change is able to take place by refocusing on the new perspectives, strategies, and possibilities for the 'coachee'.

I've seen the amazing change take place with the clients that I have had the privilege of working with and gaining their lives back, like I did mine.

I vividly remember one client who I worked with and was coaching for a period of six months. He had been working six to seven days a week and all hours. By the end of our coaching sessions, he was now having time for himself and still seeing his business grow, and having that work life balance!

---

[20] Egan, G. (2002). The Skilled Helper, a Problem- Management and Opportunity- Development Approach to Helping, United States of America: R.R. Donnelley-Crawfordsville.

Making that choice - Today's the day

Sometimes in my career I have had to make tough choices regarding the situations that I was facing, or in the lives that I was working with. Unlike some of the products that I once filled onto the shelves (like a can of baked beans) within the store, people don't fit into a product, and come in all of the same shapes and sizes. No, you just can't shut the lid down and pack them in, even when at times it could be tempting. There is the background and makeup of the individual and nationalities, and different cultures which play important roles when making decisions. There is of course, the other side, if they have breached a company policy and committed gross misconduct, and you are now having to deal with the consequences of their actions like stealing or taking drugs or drinking on the job, then you would have to respond accordingly and act wisely and fairly.

But what I'm referring to is my life choices that I can make. Today's the day to act. Have you been putting off the decision that you need to make? Today is that day for making that choice, as you don't have another tomorrow. At the start of this book, my years have flown by. I will soon be approaching my sixtieth year. Whatever I do, I want to achieve with the rest of the time I have here on planet earth. None of us is guaranteed a tomorrow. I'm so thankful that I have had the opportunity to make the right choices. Yes, some of them have been forced upon me, but I have had the good health to be able to carry them out. I want to live each day as if it were my last. Do you? Don't live with regrets.

Your Future days

"Walk with the dreamers, the believers, the courageous, the cheerful, the planners, the doers, the successful people with their heads in the clouds and their feet on the ground. Let their spirit ignite a fire within you to leave this world better than when you found it." (Wilferd Peterson[21])

As Peterson continues, *"I am walking my future days with the dreamers, the courageous and wanting to ignite a fire within all that cross my path that I will leave a legacy".*

Our future is what we make it, I have not sat back and let my terrible experience with burnout shape my future. No, I have grabbed it with both hands and aim to push forward to a new tomorrow. I am now giving others the opportunity to move out of their trapped existences and towards a new dawn. I'm so thankful for my amazing wife Pauline, for all her love and support along this journey that we have shared.

It's not been easy, and I'm determined that others can learn from my pain and heartache, so they don't have to make the same mistakes, and can potentially avoid this disease called "Burnout".

Burnout is a real epidemic within our world today, whether you agree with me or not, millions of people around the world

---

[21] Peterson, W.A. (2014) (Online). Available at https://www.passiton.com/inspirational-quotes/7340-walk-with-the-dreamers-the-believers-the/ (Accessed 17 th January 2020)

are waking up today, and suffering from its effects in some shape or form. I'm on a mission to show others that you can come out the other side to your amazing future.

Chapter Summary

- My life is so completely different and I'm on a mission.
- Seeing the difference coaching makes in people's lives.
- Utilising the Egan model Skilled Helper model[22] within coaching.
- If hope is lost it can be difficult to get it back.
- Today's the day to make that choice, as you don't have a tomorrow.
- Don't live with regrets.
- Ignite a fire to leave this world a better place.
- To your amazing future.

---

[22] Egan, G. (2002). The Skilled Helper, a Problem- Management and Opportunity- Development Approach to Helping, United States of America: R.R. Donnelley-Crawfordsville.

COACHING

I offer bespoke packages for CEO's, business leaders, companies and individuals who have been diagnosed with burnout or now recognise the warning signs and need a professional coach.

What I offer is not a therapy service, but a real and relevant package that will enable you to take charge, move forwards and regain control of your life.

It is challenging, thought provoking and involves a great deal of commitment on your behalf. If this is you, then I would be delighted to work with you.

www.mikehabbott.com

www.ingramcontent.com/pod-product-compliance
Lightning Source LLC
Chambersburg PA
CBHW050602300426
44112CB00013B/2037